Echoes and Shadows of Life

As Revealed in Folk Poetry, Old Photographs and Art

B.G. WEBB

authorHOUSE®

AuthorHouse™
1663 Liberty Drive
Bloomington, IN 47403
www.authorhouse.com
Phone: 1 (800) 839-8640

Published by AuthorHouse   03/23/2016

ISBN: 978-1-5049-7960-3 (sc)
ISBN: 978-1-5049-7959-7 (e)

Library of Congress Control Number: 2016902529

Print information available on the last page.

Any people depicted in stock imagery provided by Thinkstock are models, and such images are being used for illustrative purposes only. Certain stock imagery © Thinkstock.

This book is printed on acid-free paper.

DEDICATION

To Miss Hill who was my 5th grade teacher at Willard Grade School and my classmates. May your voices and shadows remain with me always. They are happy remembrances that I cherish.

A Truly Diverse Group of Folk

INTRODUCTION

In life we all meet interesting characters and personalities When I use the phrase "interesting characters and personalities" I'm including dogs and cats as well as human beings.

Some of these leave a positive effect on us while others leave a negative one. Some simply leave us with puzzlement. We don't quite know what to think of them.

In the following pieces I have tried to describe some of the people and pets in my life who have left a lasting impression. My descriptions of them are like echoes and shadows of the feelings I have about them.

Often when I visit antique malls, I find black and white photos with no names written on or next to them. Despite that, when I study the figures, I feel what they are expressing. Their silent communications are like the shadows on the wall --- dark, still, yet crying out their unspoken emotions.

I have included many black and white photos of people in the book. I have attempted to express what they are saying.

Finally, I've drawn sketches of people and pets and written what they are saying. It was a device used by me to highlight some of the ideas expressed in the work.

The pieces and illustrations are not in any logical order. Why? Because life isn't -- our memories of happenings aren't either.

I hope that the book will give you a laugh, make you cry and stimulate your mind. Enjoy!

TABLE OF CONTENTS

ART

WEDDINGS

"I promise to love you always."

PETS

"You give me so much T.L.C."

HAVING FUN -- 1920S

"Let's dance the Charleston."

REUNIONS

"It's so nice to be together again."

PLAY TIME -- 1930S

"Boy, do we know how to have fun."

SERVING IN THE ARMED FORCES

"This is us before and after D-Day."

WOMEN ALSO SERVED OUR COUNTRY

"This is our Delores she joined the WAVES"

GRADUATIONS

"We made it mom. You deserve to wear our caps and robes."

BROTHERS AND SISTERS

"We may have our differences, but we love each other."

CHURCH GOING

"We believe in serving the Lord"

FOLK POETRY
THE IMP WHO SPREAD
HAPPINESS EVERYWHERE

Louise was her name
    and she was the most
talented imp in God's
    universe.

Her disposition was
    not only warm but
sparkling with good
    nature and humor.

She brought joy
    to any group.
She played all the up songs
    on the piano.

She sang tunes that
    brought down the house.
Along with the song, she would
    dress up as Mae West or Marlene Dietrich.

When it came to knowledge,
    she was a wizard.
She could be astonishing
    as she gave correct answers.

When it came to wit,
    she had plenty of it.
Even Oscar Wilde would
    be jealous.

And get this,
　　　Louise could do the above
in various languages --Latin,
　　　German, French, Spanish.

When she smiled,
　　　it was as if the sky was ablaze.
It brought people to stand and
　　　clap their hands in delight.

She loved dance too.
　　　Her waltz, samba,
tango would bring a
　　　dance hall alive.

She had a delightful
　　　sense of humor.
She would smile like a risque elf
　　　as she told a joke or pulled a prank.

Yes, Louise was her name
　　　She was one in a billion.
Yes, she was the top banana
　　　of the Club Havana.

THE BLUE-COLLAR GUY WHO
WORKED FOR FORD & CO.

Herb was his name
    and he was a mechanic.
He was one smart guy
    who worked for Ford & Co.

He loved to figure out
    why cars didn't work.
He would try different approaches
    until he solved the problem.

He enjoyed disassembling the
    part that didn't work
and then go step by step to
    put it back right.

His greatest joy was
    to hear a car start up again
and sound like it was new
    and straight off the assembly line.

He worked long hours --
    even on Saturdays.
So, after he finished he often
    headed for the bars and saloons.

There he met other stiffs
    like himself
who wanted to relax over a
    beer and have a laugh.

Reading the Bible and
    believing in a loving God

weren't his things, especially after
    seeing his father die in a coal mine.

No, church-going wasn't his thing --
    nothing beat going to a tavern
to shoot darts, play pool, hear the player-piano,
    and talk with his blue-collar buddies.

On special nights there
    might be a sing-along
led by one of the bar-maids or
    Sue the owner of the joint.

And, if you wanted some forbidden
    action, there were always the
back rooms for gambling and for
    loving some "gals of the evening."

When he got home,
    he often found it mighty dull
and of course, his Mrs.
    would give him a scolding.

Herb was good to his kids.
    never beat or cussed at them
He taught them how to fish, hunt,
    drive and fix things.

In his neighborhood,
    he often became a hero
by fixing a flat and getting
    a car to start.

He never would accept pay
    for things like that.
He said, "It's not the neighborly
    thing to do."

When it came to voting,
    he only voted for candidates who
supported the blue-collar man.
    The others were S.O.B.s.

Herb was a complex man,
    didn't say much.
But he was a loving man
    in his way.

He showed his love --
    not by words,
but by the actions of
    a blue-collar working man.

He may not have had much
    fancy education,
but he was smart enough to
    get a car going again.

He found pride in having dirty
    hands, working with tools
and doing the hard jobs
    of keeping mechanical things in tune.

If he had a Bible,
    it was a fix-it-book.
If he had a God,
    it was the boss who wanted a job done.

Herb may not have run in the proper circles,
    but, in times when your car wouldn't start
you worshipped him like
    Jesus Christ himself.

ONE TOUGH COOKIE

My Grandma Della,
    was one tough gal.
While she could laugh and smile when tickled,
    She could also dish out the
tough talk and action when necessary.

She grew up on a farm
    and was used to doing tough
chores around the
    homestead.

Yes, she could milk cows,
    cut wood for the stove,
kill chickens, feed the pigs
and gather eggs from the henhouse.

She had nine children
    and learned to keep them in line
along with the skill of making
    the food (soup, etc.) stretch-out to
feed everyone.

When it came to giving advice,
    she was there with
sound, practical solutions to
    every problem.

You name it -- making a quilt,
    cooking a stew,
handling a husband, heating a home,
    planting a garden, and
of course canning, she knew what to do.

She could also be as sweet as yams covered
    with brown sugar.
She delivered babies, cared for the sick
    and dying.

THE NEIGHBORHOOD FARMER

There once was a man
    named Fred
who lived in our
    neighborhood.

He lived with his brother
    and sisters
who were all experiencing
    widowhood.

Fred managed the family
    garden along 12th Ave.
He spent most of his time
    in a small shed
working with plants and
    seeds.

He sold tomatoes and strawberries
    to the neighbors
and gave advice about
    what and how to plant
in our Victory Gardens.

Everybody loved Fred.
    He dressed in overalls
and checkered shirts.
    He always seemed so
friendly and down to earth.

One day he announced that he was going
    to live with his son in North Dakota.
We were all so sad when that day came.
    We wondered where we would get
his good advice and sweet strawberries.

"HE IS ONE HOT TACO FROM MEXICO."

You're so small -- so cute --
So handsome -- so sincere
And oh so much fun.
You have all the good things
that one hopes to find in a
Chihuahua.

    Taco, Taco you're so dear.

How we admire your golden brown fur.
How we love your white underside and bib.
And what a striking face you have!
You seem to be wearing a white mask.

    Taco, Taco you're so gorgeous.

Your big brown eyes reveal your
Inner personality -- your desire to love and please us.
They reflect your high I.Q. and intelligence too.
They also reveal your love of games and fun.

    Taco, Taco you're so admirable

Your large pointed ears are up for action.
Your tiny wet nose and upturned mouth
give you an impish look.
You seem to be smiling at the world --
so full of good humor.

    Taco, Taco you're so cute.

You walk with so much confidence.
Your tail is usually curved high over your back.

You have such pose too.
And, when it comes to facing a camera, you appear
to be willing and able.

Taco, Taco you have such a presence.

We adore your need to lick us in the morning to wake us up.
We laugh as we feel your tongue in our ears --
it tickles us so.
Your need to be picked up and hugged only adds
to your loving nature.
Your need to tease us with your many antics brings joy to our lives.

Taco, Taco you are so warm and outgoing.

We've gotten used to the sounds you make.
Your whimpering, growling and yapping noises
not only give you the attention you desire, but
force us to keep alert to your every whim.

Taco, Taco you are such an attention-getter.

We marvel at how curious you are.
You look into the dishwasher, the refrigerator.
You know when we load the washer and unload the dryer.
You look out windows to see who is coming and going.
For some reason you feel that they are all coming
to see you --- hence the need to open the door and look out.
You sit by the door to listen for the sounds of
passersby. Of course, you believe that they are
There to see you.

Taco, Taco you are so inquisitive -- such a busybody.

You can be so playful -- so mischievous.
We have learned to guard our socks and slippers.
We have taken care not to drop anything on the floor.

We know that your biggest thrill is to grab something
so you can have the pleasure of someone chasing you.

Taco, Taco you're such a prankster.

You have forced us to change.
We no longer put the toilet paper on the spool.
We have purchased taller waste baskets.
We watch where we put our purses and wallets.
We placed our pots of artificial flowers on high stands
because you love to seize them and run off.
We make sure our napkins are out of your reach.
Indeed, even Clarence our large stuffed toy lion is
now sitting on a chair and out of danger of being
grabbed by you.

Taco, Taco you keep us on our toes.

You make us more aware of puppy behavior.
You chew a lot because your teeth are coming in.
You seize things because of your natural hunting instincts.
You lead with your mouth in self-defense.
Your fast running is due to your youthful energy.
Your reactions to knocks at the door and strangers
reveal your feelings of getting used to your new surroundings.
Taco, Taco you can be such a challenge.

You certainly are a macho little guy.
Let's face it you do have a big "dick."
You were bred to be a stud.
You have such an interest in "private parts"
-- and "bathroom activities."
We certainly have learned not to bend over
when you are around.
We have seen you have sexual relations with your
stuffed toy bear.

    Taco, Taco you're so sexy.

You enjoy simple pleasures.
You like to go to sleep on the back of the living room chair.
You enjoy playing with your toys -- especially the bear.
You like being taken for a walk at the mall.
You like to go for a drive in the country.
You love going under the sofa to explore and to
hide under the bed when we use the vacuum cleaner.h
    Taco, Taco you know how to enjoy life.

Oh Taco, we love you so.
Despite your hang-ups and feisty ways,
We adore you. Why?
Because you make us laugh --
and keep us on our toes.
You give us something to care for --
something to get up for.

    Taco, Taco we think you're just about it.

Many thanks for all you do for us

    Taco, Taco you will always be our little friend.

MISS THUNDER AND LIGHTNING

She taught at Moline High and
    she did it with fire and brimstone.

Public speaking and acting
    were what she lived for.

She could become so dramatic
    when she read lines from a play or poem.

You learned never to cross her
    because she was capable of
saying deadly put-downs.

Yes, indeed, she was quite a gal.
    One thing for sure,
you never forgot her,
    even though she wasn't your pal.

Putting on plays were
    a delight to her.
She loved to direct and be
    in command.

I don't think they make
    teachers like Miss Garst --
she was one of a kind --
    unique
             and unforgettable

THE MAN KNOWN FOR SAYING
"SHIT HAPPENS"

My Uncle Chester was such
    an attractive man.
He was tall,
    with thick wavy hair
and blue eyes and a
    wonderful smile.
He didn't have a lot of education.
    He was well-spoken and seem to know
a lot but it came from the
    school of hard knocks.

His favorite phrase was
    "shit happens!"
Why? Because according to him
    life is very unpredictable.

Instead of relying on a kind
    Father in Heaven,
he told me that one must rely
    on oneself and the
kindness of strangers.

If life throws you a curve,
    you had to take it
and move on. You had to hold on
    until things changed.

As a kid, I didn't really buy into it.
    I thought that if one plans, studies,
takes care, one could avoid trouble.
    Nothing bad would happen to you
if you were good.

But, as I lived life,
    I found out that
my uncle was right.
    Life is unpredictable.
Shit happens. Bad things
    happen to good people.

So, I learned to rely on
    myself and if I was
lucky a kind stranger
    would be willing
to help me.

TWO LADIES FROM SWEDEN

They lived in an upstairs apartment
    in our neighborhood.
Both had come from Sweden
    many years ago.

One we called "Grandma Johnson"
    because she was so old.
She lived above her son and
    his wife Nora.

She helped bring in money
    by making bradded oval rugs
from pieces of cloth given
    to her by neighbors.

The rugs were very colorful
    and sold fast.
People used them in their kitchens
    and liked thinking of the lady from Sweden.

Like the rugs, Grandma Johnson
    was colorful, strong and
represented the pioneer
    spirit that had made this country.

She shared her small apartment
    with her sister Karla
who was old too but still strong
    enough to earn some money.

She cleaned offices in
    downtown
usually in the late afternoon
    or at night.

The neighbors loved her because
   despite being tired from work,
she was always ready with a smile
   and an offer to help.

We called her "Aunt Karla" because
   she seemed like family
when we talked about our ups and
   downs with life.

Well, they are both gone
   now. But all remember that
they fit the phrase "good neighbors"
   to a Tee.

KELLY THE MAVERICK

We once had a neighbor
        named Kelly
who was well-known for
        being a handful.

He wasn't much to look at --
        had a bald head
and only stood 5'5"
        from head to toe.

He always dressed in
        overalls
and blue work shirts
        and work shoes.

What he lacked in
        appearance
he made up for in
        his strong persona.

He had strong opinions
        which he uttered
in strong language.
        Indeed, hell and shit
were often used by him.

He worked at John Deere Co.
        on the assembly line.
He was a blue-collar
        worker,
and he was proud of that --
        and often said so.

He was a union man and
    liked to say nasty things
about the big shots
    who wanted to undermine
the rights of labor.

He disliked politicians --
    all of them.
Republicans, Democrats, Independents--
    Kelly didn't like them.

Why?
    Well, he said that they were
all dishonest and out for
    themselves.

He also didn't believe in
    religious groups -- or
for that matter
    God.

He once said that "when your dead, you're
    dead. There isn't any Heaven or Hell.
--- that we are just another species
    on this planet with no real purpose."

He liked to get drunk
    and yell his opinions
throughout the neighborhood
    until someone usually shouted,
"Kelly, go home and get to bed."

Now, there was one soft spot in his nature.
    What?
Well, it was animals -- especially dogs.
    He had a pet dog named Pal.
He loved that dog.

You often saw them
    going up the alley --
walking or running together.
    It was quite a sight
to see Kelly with a smile on his face.

So, Kelly may have seemed obnoxious
    to many,
but, to dog lovers he showed a side of himself that
    caused them to believe that he

    may be right on a lot
of other things too.

THE TERROR OF WILLARD GRADE SCHOOL

Miss Swanson was our musical
    commander-in-chief.
Some called her
    "the terror of Willard."

She had been there the
    longest and thus
insisted upon being treated
    with awe and respect.

To be in her 6th grade class
    was considered to be a
time of being obedient.
    She was the Queen Bee.

When she conducted
    musical assemblies,
she used a whistle
    to get our attention.

She also used a harmonica to
    help the singers
start on the right
    note.

She was in charge of the
    boys who helped
keep the street safe from
    on-coming traffic

Miss Swanson (nicknamed "Swannie")
    would line up the Safety Patrol
for inspection and then assign
    them to their positions.

One has to admit she had quite a persona.
    One thing for sure,
You made sure you always obeyed her
    and never crossed her.

Why? Because you would get the
    scolding of your life.
You knew that once you crossed her,
    you had made an enemy for life.

And that, my dear reader is why she was
    called "The Terror of Willard."
They don't make gals like her anymore,
    and perhaps it is just as well.

But, if we don't have
    colorful characters like her,
what would we write
    poetry about?

THE LADY WITH THE CARING HEART

Irene was her name
 and she represented old values.
She believed in self-sacrifice
 and coming to the need of others.

While she wasn't beautiful
 with her cubby figure and
her round face,
 she possessed a caring spirit
that radiated from her warm smile.

She would answer the call
 of those in danger.
She would give you a kind word and
 lots of T.L.C. when needed.

She worked hard raising her sister
 after their mother died.
She did the household chores from
 washing to ironing to putting
coal into the furnace.

Irene was gifted --
 she played the old upright piano
and sang in the church choir and
 made crocheted table cloths

If you needed help
 with your Latin or math,
Irene was right there to
 teach you step by step.

I wish we had more
 Irenes.
We need more people who care
 and put others before themselves.

MISS CONFIDENCE PERSONIFIED

Margaret was her name
    but everyone called her Maggie.
She was petite and
    always dressed up like a queen.

She developed a persona
    of radiant confidence
and savoir faire on the job
    and everywhere.

As a sales lady she could sell
    anything from stockings to
girdles to underwear
    with savvy.

When she presided over
    her Eastern Star Chapter,
she did it with ease and
    great style.

Yes, indeed, Maggie made sure
    the usual business was
handled quickly and that money
    projects were undertaken.

Honored quests were welcomed
    warmly and then taken
to meet the Worthy Matron in
    the East.

Yes, she was one grand gal.
    She looked like a queen
and got the job done
    with speed and style.

THE COUPLE WHO LOVED EACH OTHER AND THEIR NEIGHBORS

Arvid and Caroline were
        their names
and they worked at the
        Good Estate.

He was the butler
        to the master
while she was the head maid.

They did their jobs
        with great finesse
and were rewarded
        with money and an
apartment.

Every winter they went
        with their "Good Family"
to enjoy their beach mansion
        in sunny Florida.

They loved each other
        with a passion
but they took the time
        to reach out to their
neighbors.

If anyone was in danger,
        they were there.
If anyone needed a helping hand,
        they were there.

Even when they were in Florida,
    they didn't forget
their friends in Moline or
    Davenport.

Oh no, they sent many
    coconuts and
boxes of pineapples
    and oranges.

When they celebrated their
    50th wedding anniversary,
all the neighbors came to see
    them cut their cake and
dance the rumba.

THE PURPLE LADY

We had a neighbor
    whose name was Mertle.
She had a passion for
    all things purple.

When she got dressed up,
    she only wore purple.
Yes, she had purple
    stockings, dresses, hats,
gloves and even shoes that
    were purple.

When she put her clothes
    out to dry,
everyone found out that
    she owned underpants
and slips that were
    -- you guessed it --
    purple.

It was well-known among
    the guys in town
that Mertle never wore a
    girdle.

She flirted with men
    because she was very
sexy and also because she
    was so fertile.

She drove a Packard
    which was of course purple.
It helped advertise her
    beauty salon
name The Lady Purple.

It's slogan was: Abra-cadabra and
    You Too Will Be as Gorgeous
as The Purple Lady.

A MAFIA MEMBER?

I had a roommate named
    Mike Grosso
Who was as strong and tough
    as a boxer.

He came from Chicago --
    north side and
it was believed that his
    father was a Don.

Mike was 5'9" and
    weighed in at
180. His favorite place
    was the gym.

He worked on his muscles --
    especially in his arms
and abs. After a work out
    he got pleasure out of
soaping his balls.

Being social wasn't his
    strong point.
He liked to be alone
    and order others around.

In winter he gave the impression
    of a tough Mafia hood.
He never wore a hat
    over his crewcut.

His coat was made of black leather.
    He always wore the collar up

to add to the effect of saying:
    "I'm a tough hood from the
Italian neighborhood."

He demanded respect or
    you got his fist in your face
or up your ass
    if he really got mad.

It might surprise you but
    he went to Mass and Confession
regularly. He always was tough
    on Catholics who didn't
follow the rules.

I think to him the Pope was the
    head of the family -- and
you gave him respect and
    obedience.

He often said that he was
    in favor of the death penalty
and public whippings for those
    who did not live up to the
10 Commandments.

As his roommate I was
    told what to do and when and how.
After a semester, I moved out.
    I felt as if I was being held
hostage by a hood of the mob.

I don't know what happened to Mike
    but I have to admit
he was one tough cookie --
    and a son of a bitch.

Perhaps he is serving time in a prison
    or being a capo of the mob or
perhaps he replaced his father as Don.
    Who knows he may have become a
priest and later a bishop.
    I'm only sure of one thing,
I'm glade I'm not his roommate.

WHY DID IT HAPPEN TO FRANKIE?

Frankie was such a beauty
    with her radiant smile
and gorgeous figure
    which she displayed with pose.

Oh God, why Frankie?

She had the most lovely sounding voice
    that gave one reassurance.
And, her laughter would light up a room
    with warmth and joy.

Oh Heavenly Father, why Frankie?

She had a caring heart
    which she showed in her
devotion to those in need of
    emotional support.

Oh Almighty One, why Frankie?

She was helping friends
    when it happened.
Off for a short outing to
    celebrate their friendship.

Oh Jesus, why Frankie?

Then he attacked them,
    tied them up,
beat them before he
    raped them.

41

Oh Christ, why Frankie?

When her body was found in the snow,
      she was bound with ropes.
Her beautiful face was gone,
      replaced with blood and bone fragments

Oh Father in Heaven, why Frankie?

Why do bad things happen
      to good people like Frankie?
Why wasn't she protected by
      a caring Father in Heaven?

Why? Why? Why?

Do you exist dear Lord?
      When people pray are you there?
Did we create you to give us comfort
      in this brutal world?

Oh great Mighty One, why Frankie?
      Why dear, caring Frankie?

THE GAL WHO LOVED HORSES

Nobody ever had a better
    childhood friend than Carol.

She was cute and loved to dress up
    in the latest fashions.

She introduced me to the
    Saturday matinee at the
Roxy theatre.

There we would join other kids
    to eat popcorn and see
two westerns and the
    serial.

We joined other kids in booing
    at the villain who was
giving Roy Rogers a rough
    way to go.

We loved to cheer when Roy and
    his horse Trigger came to
the rescue of the lady in
    distress.

Carol's passion for horses was
    so intense that she often
went to the local stables
    to ride them.

Her dream was to own a horse
    of her own.
Her father said he would buy one

if she could find a place to
board it.

I went with Carol to see if
    Mr. Swan who owned a barn
would be willing to
    board her horse for a fee.

Alas, he refused her request.
    So, she continued to go to
Western films and to the stables
    to enjoy her love of horses.

Later, she moved away from
    my neighborhood.
But, one day she showed up
    with a horse.

She let me ride him and then said
    "Good bye."
I never saw her again. But, the image
    of her riding off remains with me.
And, also the joy that Carol
    finally owned a horse.

THE MAN WHO LIKED TO HIDE

There was a man named
    Aaron Solomann who
liked to hide behind a
    proper persona.

He had a lot to hide.
    Not only did he come from
a poor blue-collar family in Brooklyn,
    he was also a Jew.

In those days
    it was bad to be one.
They were viewed as Christ-killers.

They faced all kinds
    of obstacles.
They couldn't't own land,
    They were barred
from clubs.

If they were orthodox,
    they were targets of jokes,
ridicule and even
    physical attacks.

Aaron met the
    hostile situation
by changing himself to fit
    in with the population.

How? you ask.
    By reinventing himself.
He changed name. He became
    Arnold Smith.

He no longer attended
      the synagogue.
Instead he joined the
      Episcopalians.

By starting out as a clerk
      in a law practice,
he eventually passed
      the bar exam.

By this time he
      had disciplined himself
not to use phases
      in Yiddish.

If he went to the gym
      and someone saw that he
was circumcised, he said he
      had it done for sanitation purposes.

Yes indeed, he created a
      proper persona to the public.
He was a born again Christian who
      came from Nebraska.

He joined many
      Masonic groups --
the Blue Lodge, White Shrine
      Eastern Star and True Kindred.

If he did run into a few Jews,
      he made it his business not to
even recognize a menorah and the
      celebration of Rosh Ha Shanah.

When it came to marriage,
      he only dated girls from the

Junior League and others who were
    as WASP as you can wish.

Yes, Aaron or should I say Arnold
    pulled it off.
He succeeded in hiding
    his Jewishness.

In his defense he would say: "Hey,
    you got to do what you got to do.
It's a tough world out there. Bad things
    happen to good people and that includes
Jews."

HE LOVED ACTING ON STAGE AND IN LIFE

Tyrone was quite
    an actor.
He could play Blanche in Williams'
    Streetcar Named Desire.

He could do Shakespeare
    too.
He loved to play Romeo
    as well as King Lear.

But the best parts
    he had were in life --
playing the professor,
    the husband and even the wife.

He liked to hide
    behind roles.
Give him a costume
    and he was in heaven.

Why? Because he could
    hide his real self.
Nobody knew who he really was
    including himself.

Now, once in a while someone
    would catch on.
They would know he wasn't who he seemed and
    were being treated as fools.

It didn't happen often.
   He was clever to create a
public persona that seemed
   proper but also exciting.

In his mind there wasn't
   anything as good as acting.
He could become all sorts
   and still hide himself.

ONE SMART GUY

I knew a guy who
    was as smart as a whip.
You name it, and he knew it
    or where you could find out.

He was great at team work.
    He loved to solve problems
by working with others.
    The more complex the topic,
the better.

    He kept up with the news and
all current topics.
    He subscribed to all sorts of
publications.

    He had a great sense of humor
He liked puns, jokes, one-liners.
    Of course he liked naughty humor
and jokes about bodily functions.

    Yes, any story that pertained
to shit and the butt-hole
    was greeted with belly laughs and
giggling.

    Now he kept that part of his
personality under cover.
    It was reserved for people like himself
who enjoyed raunchy humor.

When it came to business, he always
    presented a warm, smart persona.
It pleased the clients who depended upon
    his expertise to solve their problem.

Yes, he was one smart guy --
    so professional -- so savvy on the outside
and yet underneath was an elf
    ready to get into mischief
and have some fun.

THE FRAGILE LADY WITH A SMILE

She welcomed everyone with
    a smile
It glowed like a neon
    welcoming sign.

She loved to teach
    Bible School and
use a flannel
board to
    tell stories from the Bible.

She had a passion for the
    story of Noah
and his ark and the manger
    scene in Bethlehem.

She read her Bible everyday
    and prayed to the Almighty
to protect those
    she loved.

She was known for her
    "little poems"
that she sent to so many
    who were in need.

Her deep devotion was also found
    in the role of motherhood.
She loved to design and sew
    little outfits for her boys.

And could she cook!
    Her pie crust was so light
and her homemade chicken noodles
    would melt in your mouth.

However, she was defenseless
    against the brutal forces.
Tears would come into her eyes
    as she felt abandoned,
isolated and maligned.

She often denied or hid
    from the harsh realities of life.
She didn't know how to meet them
    except pray and retreat.

She was a woman who possessed
    great beauty
but one who took refuge within
    herself in the face of abuse.

She was like a pink rose
    that blooms in the sunshine.
She radiated joy when told that
    she was special.

But when the cold winds of
    hostility came her way,
she shivered and withered
    until she died away.

Dorothy was her name
    and we hope she is
in heaven surrounded
    by angels singing "Hallelujah."

THE POPCORN LADY

There was a lady in our neighborhood named
    Mrs. Applegate.

She invited me over every time her granddaughter visited.
    Her name was Katie.

As we would glide back and forth on the swing that
    was on the front porch, we smiled and giggled.

Why you ask?
    Because we knew that Mrs. Applegate was making
    popcorn in the kitchen.

I can hear it now — Pop! Pop! Pop!

And the smell --- Wow! Wow! Wow!

It was the best popcorn ever -- even better than
    what they sold at the Roxy movie theatre.

Why? Because it was fresh and came from the
    Applegate farm outside our town.

When she served it to us in large bowls, she put
    plenty of butter on it.

Oh, how I would like to visit Katie again on that
    front porch --- swing and eat that wonderful popcorn.

ODE TO PEGGY SUE

Oh you look so cute
    with your black spots
situated in all the
    right places.

Yes, those black ears,
    tail and paws
contrast so well against
    your white fur.

    Peggy Sue, you're adorable.

However, you don't
    realize one important thing.
You are a dog
    and not a human being.

You sleep in our bed
    and have the run of the house.
You wouldn't recognize a
    dog's bed if you saw one.

    Peggy Sue, you're mixed up.

But, you were born under
    the sign of Gemini.
So, no wonder you're
    confused and display
two personalities.

We are partly to blame
    since we call you by so
many names. Yes, we call you

"Lady Margaret, "Madam"
and even "Royal Highness".
 So, no wonder you have an
identity problem.

 Peggy Sue, you need a psychiatrist.

Perhaps you think you are
 a human because you are
so very smart. Granted, you
 have a large vocabulary.

Here are some words that you
 recognize:

 "popcorn"

 "outside"

 "leash"

 "bye-bye"

 "get into the car"

 "nap time"

 "let's play ball"

 Peggy Sue, you are very smart.

We know that the passions of
 your life are:
Pretending someone is after you
 and you go under the bed
and bark like crazy.

The other thing you love is
    to go in the car.
You look out the windows,
    and hope we will go to a
fast-food drive-in where you will
    be given a snack.

Peggy Sue, you are so much fun.

Peggy Sue, we love you dear. You're not
    perfect, but we aren't either.
You love us unconditionally and only
    ask for a hug, a treat and
a belly-rub.

Peggy Sue, you're so special.

WHY DID IT HAPPEN TO KEN?

Ken seemed to have it all.
    He had a good paying job
at a local foundry
    with a pension plan.

His wife was a beautiful
    outgoing gal.
who had given him two
    children and plenty of support.

When it came to church,
    he was there every Sunday.
He believed that Jesus
    was the Son of God.

He read the Bible too
    and prayed to the Almighty
for the souls of others
    and for the recovery of the sick.

Then he was killed
    at work.
As he was returning to his work bench,
    a heavy piece of steel fell on his head.

All were stunned.
    They asked, "Why oh why did
this happen to Ken?"
    Oh Jesus, why him?"

His wake was so sad.
    There was Ken in his casket.
There was the grieving widow
    and her crying children.

All wondered why God Almighty
    had allowed this to happen.
Even the minister couldn't explain
    why bad things happen to good people.

Even today people remember Ken
    and ask the same questions.
Even today they realize what was
    taken away from him.

He never saw his children
    grow up.
He never enjoyed the company
    of his beloved wife.

Why dear Lord did you take him?
    Did you need him more
than his family and wife?
    Why oh Heavenly Father, oh why?

A LOVE POEM TO MARLENE DIETRICH

Oh how I love thee
    Marlene
My heart and soul
    lie at your feet.

You were so sexy
    in The Blue Angel
and so erotic in
    Blonde Venus.

Your beauty is both
    gorgeous and mysterious
as seen in so many of
    your films.

Yet, you can be quite an
    imp and comedienne
as seen in
    Destry Rides Again.

Oh, how I love to hear your
    low voice
sing songs of amore
    such as "I'm Falling in Love Again."

Oh, how I admire your courage.
    You left your beloved Berlin
to defy Hitler and
    support the Allied cause.
I admire your habit of
    cross-dressing
to reveal your love of
    both men and women.

There will never be
    another like you.
I'll always remember you
    when I hear "Lili Marlene."

AN ODE TO YOUNG HERBY DALE

You are such a
    handsome guy.
You look like
    Cary Grant.

No wonder all
    the girls
have a crush
    on you.

You have so many
    talents too.
You can play the trumpet
    and croon like Frank Sinatra.

When it comes
    to diving
you put on
    quite an act.

You look like
    Tarzan
in your G-string
    swim trunks.

When you dive
all eyes are on
you and of course
    your "Package"
And can you dance!
    Wow, at the REC
you "cut the rug"
    with the best.

You're good at
    playing pool
and talking
    guy talk.

But you're an
    independent cuss.
But that's part of
    your charm.

You like to go
    your own way
and do your
    own thing.

But you love
    to give others a ride
in the car
    that you drive.
"Climb aboard," you say
    and they do
because they enjoy
    being on wheels with
Herby Dale.

You're quite a guy
    --so much charm
and wit,
    so full of fun and
mischief.

No wonder,
    despite your flaws
most think you're
    our Clark Gable
from Gone With The Wind.

THE FOREIGN STUDENT FROM INDIA

Jawaharial was his name
    and he came from
Benares, India.

I met him when I opened
    the door to my room
at the dorm.

He seemed to be a very
    exotic personage
who had stepped out of
    some novel about India.

He was a tall, lean and
    muscular guy
who had dark skin and
    a mustache.

He greeted me with a warm
    smile that radiated
a lot of intelligence
    and self-esteem.

He wore a turban in which
    he stored his long hair.
He looked directly at me
    as he introduced himself.

He spoke without an accent
    having gone to one
of the best private schools
    in India.

We were uncomfortable
    with each other for some time.
He was a devoted Hindu
    while I was a Presbyterian.

He often spoke about
    life along the Ganges River
and all the holy events
    that took place in his
home town of Benares.

We often argued about
    religion.
Was Jesus or Vishnu the true
    representative of God or
Brahma?

While I defended the <u>Bible</u>
    as the true word,
Jawaharial defended the <u>Bhagavad Gita</u>
    as being more embracing
of truth.

At first, he seemed
    devoted to his heritage.
He attended religious services
    with other Indian students.

He often spoke of his beloved
    mother and stressed
that he only wanted to date
    Indian girls on campus.

He often complained about how
    Americans viewed him as a
poorly educated Negro.

He felt that Americans knew
       little about the great culture
of his country and that they
       were very materialistic.

Then, one day, I noticed
       a big change.
He stopped mixing with
       other Indian students.

He had his hair cut
       and started wearing
western styles of
       clothes and shoes.

He became very attracted to
       blonde American girls.
They seemed to be so unusual
       and exotic to him.

As we talked now, the
       conversation often turned
into who was getting the most
       from the girls we were
dating.

Then, something happened that
       completely changed our relationship.
Late one night as I was sleeping
       I woke up to find someone in bed
with me -- Jawaharial.

He held me tightly as I at first
       resisted intimate contact.
Then -smiling- he reached down and
       gently fondled my ass and penis.

I responded by finding myself
    enjoying every touch.
His black skin was as smooth as silk
    and his fondling showed the
skill of a masseur.

I'll admit that I had encountered
    similar situations before.
As a Cub Scout I had gone out for
    a week at the Boy Scout Camp.

There I learned more than how to
    tie different knots.
I had found out what the boys
    did at the midnight swims
at the pool.

I joined the guys in taking off
    my swim trunks to swim naked.
I found myself being touched
    and pawed by the older boys.

When I went to have a shower,
    I found the older guys
forming a circle and then
    having a good time masturbating.

So, I didn't resist much as Jawaharial
    held me in his arms.
He helped me come and then he turned
    me over and came between my thighs.

However, Jawaharial's move on me changed
    my life forever.
I felt attracted not only to women
    but to men.

We continued to date girls,
      compare notes and to have
passionate sex sessions for
      the next two years.

After graduation, Jawaharial got a
      good job with an international firm,
married a nice Hindu girl, had
      a mistress -- blonde of course -- and
fathered a large family.

After graduation, I got teaching jobs,
      married a wonderful intelligent woman
and joined all the right social
      clubs and organizations.

But, in terms of sex, I found myself
      always remembering those passionate
sessions with Jawaharial. And, I must admit,
      that while I did not love him,
I had the best sex with the man from
      Benares.

"IT'S ALL ABOUT GENES BABY."

A friend of mine
    who has a brilliant mind
doesn't believe in helping
    anyone in a bind.

As a scientist
    she views life
purely as
    an anthropologist.

According to her, every
    species has a way
to eliminate the genetically
    weak and unfit.

By doing this
    the weak genes
will be quickly on their way
    down nature's Ganges.

Only the species
    called humans
think it is o.k.
    to help the weak.

She finds that so sad
    because it only leads to
an increase in idiots
    and bone heads.

And that's why we see
    overpopulation, hunger
and wars for food,
    goods and land.

When Christmas comes around
    she never drops a bill
into the Salvation Army's
    many kettles.

Once I asked her if she
    would make an exception
if the person was poor but
    showed some smarts.

She thought for a moment
    and then said, "Yes I would
help him/her, but she/he would
    have to be really smart.

When it came to religion,
    she took a scientific view.
Mankind created a God
    in order to survive.

She believed that humans
    evolved
and weren't given a clue
    as to why they are here.

In desperation they
    created religions to explain things.
They needed answers, rules
    and comfort in bad times.

She was tolerant to those
    who prayed and believed
in a caring God.
    She said, "If it gives them comfort,
let them have it."

For her a scientific view
     was satisfactory.
She was content to wait until
     research gave the answers.

She keeps her views
     to herself.
She doesn't want to be
     done in by do--gooders.

Yes, she fears that
     they will attack her.
Then, the species will be out
     a genetically strong
person — herself.

THE MAIDEN LADY AND THE OVERSOUL

Miss Warner was the
    maiden lady in our neighborhood.

Born to people of the upper class,
    she was sent to college
to be educated.

While she was tall and slim,
    and had gorgeous red hair
and a glowing complexion,
she was never courted
    by a gentleman caller.

She remained unmarried
    and taught scores of students
in the 4th grade
    at Garfield Grade School.

When she retired she
    was asked to care for her aged
uncle in his large home on 12th Avenue.
    She accepted out of
loyality to her family.

She managed the estate
    very well --
hired maids, wash ladies
    and gardeners.

She didn't go to church.
    Why? Because she found
comfort in the
    world of nature.

She filled her home with
    plants and flowers.
She loved walking along the
    trails in the nearby woods.

There she united with the
    spirit of the Oversoul.
It was all around her --
    in the trees, the birds,
the rabbits and especially
    in the clouds in the sky.

In the winter she fed the
    birds and she put out
food for the squirrels and
    the chipmunks.

While she was remembered for
    her efficient ways,
we grew to love her for her
    love of nature and
special union with the
    Oversoul.

A LITTLE BROTHER'S POEM
TO HIS BIG BROTHER

My name is Buddy
 and I have
an older brother
 named Herby.

I always have
 to look up to him
because he's seven years older
 and much taller.

Herby likes to tell me
 what to do,
when to do it and
 how to do it.

If we play together
 in our room,
he directs me in making
 airplanes and log-cabins.

When we were much younger,
 we shared the same bed
and had fun having
 pillow fights.

We compete for mom's
 attention and
bug each other over all
 kinds of things.

When he has his
 friends over,

he doesn't wish to
    share them.

Oh no, he tells me
    to "go away,"
and in some cases
    "to get lost."

At other times
    when we are alone,
he likes to amuse me
    and make me laugh.

He makes funny faces
    like a monkey
and shares his candy bar
    with me.

In a way, he feels
    I'm his pet.
I become a doggie on
    a leash.

I am in awe
    of him.
Why? Because he can
    do so many things.

He goes out to the
    Boy Scout Camp.
He can play the trumpet
    and swim like a dolphin.

I can't do much.
    I like to direct
neighborhood circuses.
    I can make up stories
that give kids nightmares.

I'm not bad at
      kick-ball
and making and flying
      kites.

I like going to the
      movies with my
friend Carol and listening
      to "Captain Midnight."

But, I often wish I
      could be like Herby.
Kids like him for his
      charm and wit.

But that never will be.
      I seem to be an
observer -- someone on the
      outside looking in.

I like to be alone deep
      in the woods or
in a self-made winter
      camp.

Life has something else
      in store for me --
maybe just looking and
      observing.
Meanwhile, I'll try to
      enjoy being Herby's
puppy. I'll sit up and
      wag my tail when he
finds the time for me.

THE STRAY CAT NAMED BABY

He came at night --
    around 7:00 P.M.
As he walked passed our
    porch, he seemed lost.

He meowed and looked at
    us as if asking, "Do you have some
food to give me?" Then, he
    meowed again and again.

Mom said, "He looks like
    a stray young alley cat."
I replied, "I'll get him something
    to eat."

As I went upstairs to get some
    lunch meat, mom picked up
the little kitty with the white face
    and the black tiger stripes.

When I came down with the food,
    the kitty ate it quickly
while maintaining its pose and persona.

"Can I keep him mom, he looks
    like he needs a home."
"Sure Buddy, if that's what
    you want."

"You understand that you're
    going to be the one to
look after him. You will let him
    in and out and feed him."

"Oh, I will mom! I think I'll
        call him Baby because that's
what he is going to be to me --
        my little baby."

So Baby came to live
        with us and in a way
took care of me as much
        as I cared for him.

He would lay on my bed
        while I did my homework.
He would listen to the radio program
        along with me too.

He would alert us to
        any stranger in the house.
He would warm us of danger;
        he became our sentinel.

He loved to be petted
        and have his belly rubbed.
He would meow with
        contentment to our gentle touches.

He insisted on going out
        all night for his escapades.
In the morning he would return
        and loudly meow for his meal.

Then, there came a day
        when he didn't return.
We never did find out
        what happened to Baby.

We were sad for a long time.
        Baby had been our protector,

our pal, our friend.
    We kept listening for meowing.

Oh Baby, where ever you are now,
    we want you to know that we still miss you.
You gave us more TLC than
    most people we know.

We will always cherish the memory
    of that night when a little kitten
came meowing at us.
    Baby, you stayed a long time with us
before you went on your journey.

THE MAN WHO SAT IN THE WRONG PEW

Mr. Wood was his name
    and he got into trouble
because of all things,
    he sat in the wrong pew.

He had come from a
    farm family
that had settled in
    a town outside Moline.

He and his siblings
    were all successful.
He went into law
    while the others farmed.

His sisters all married
    well -- business men,
teachers, lawyers and
    even doctors.

Mr. Wood became a
    leader in his town
and the owner of many
    apartments.

After he and his siblings
    lost their spouses,
he invited them to share his
    large home.

They all agreed
    and loved being
together again as
    they had on the farm.

They put on parties
      for the renters,
fireworks for the 4th of July,
      and pumpkins and cider
for Halloween.

The kids in the neighborhood
      loved Mr. Wood.
He would wave at them
      as he drove his '39 Buick.

Then it happened,
      the event at stirred up
discussion and gossip.
      Mr. Wood sat in the wrong pew.

One Sunday he decided
      to go to church.
It had been some time since
      he had been there.

He drove to the church
      and took a seat in a pew
--up close so he could
      hear the sermon.

He joined in as the
      congregation sang
"Jesus Loves Me" and
      "Onward Christian soldiers."

Several days later,
      he received a letter
reprimanding him for
      sitting in the wrong pew.

Well, you can imagine his
    surprise and shock.
He and his siblings had supported
    the church for years.

They often didn't attend
    services because of their
advancing years and
    difficulty in hearing and seeing.

He tried speaking to the minister
    but didn't get much sympathy.
All the neighbors thought it was terrible
    and sided with Mr. Wood.

He finally resigned from the church.
    He wrote that even Jesus Christ
himself would never go there if one
    had to sit in the right pew.

A TRUE BELIEVER IN A CARING
HEAVENLY FATHER

When I was ten years old
    I had a Sunday School teacher
named Mrs. Bailey.

As a girl she had been sent
    to a Christian Academy
where she met her husband who
    became a minister.

She believed that faith and
    prayer were the
answers to life's problems.

She believed in a caring
    loving God who was our
Father in Heaven.

Redemption came by believing
    that He sent his son Jesus
to die for our sins
    on the cross.
We needed only to believe
    in that to be saved.

She told us that everyday
    she set aside a time
to pray to the Almighty
    to help those in need.

But, she said that
    in order to meet the problems,

the Heavenly Father needed our
help by actually doing
something about it.

During church services she added
lots of drama.
While the choir sang or when
the minister gave his sermon,
she would cry out "Amen! Amen!"
or "Hallelujah! Hallelujah!."
She raised money to help our missionaries
in far-off Africa.
She visited the sick in homes and hospitals.
She provided food baskets for the needy.

As a student in her class,
I have to admit she was very convincing.
She practiced what she preached.
She often said, "You must take action to
live up to The Golden Rule."

MR. INDEPENDENT

He taught U.S. History and Business Law,
    and his name was Mr. Nyquist.

He was well known throughout
    the school for being an
independent son of a gun.

True, he was full of himself
    but boy could he teach.

He had several degrees
    and knew his subjects well.
You name it,
    he knew it.

Since he was fresh from the military service,
    he was worldly and
very down to earth in his delivery.

Yes, he had experienced the
    real world where a lot of
bad things happen to good
    people.

Now, he did have a sense of fun,
    but it could be hard to take
without a glass of rum.

Once he gave us a pop quiz and then
    at the end smiled and shouted,
"April Fool's Day!"

Yes, he was quite a corker but
    we learned a lot of history
and a lot about the realities of life.
    We also had a lot of fun wondering
what surprises he had in store for us
    in the future.

I hope they still have teachers
    like Mr. Nyquist around.
You learn a lot and make learning
    fun and exciting.

Let's face it, it helps to learn
    when you have a colorful
teacher with an exciting
    persona.

A LOVE POEM TO TENNESSEE

Oh how I would adore
    to make love to you.
Oh, how I want to embrace you
    to show you that I understand your pain.

Ever since I saw <u>The</u> <u>Glass</u> <u>Menagerie</u>,
    I felt a strong kinship with you.
I too grew up with such a
    family as yours.

I can relate to a child
    becoming an observer --
someone always being on the outside
    looking in.

I too was touched
    by those in torment
and often found myself escaping into
    a world of fantasy.

You explore so many of the
    brutal aspect of the human condition.
In <u>Sweet</u> <u>Bird</u> <u>of</u> <u>Youth</u> you show us
    what is behind the curtains.

I, like you, found outlets
    in writing and in the arts.
I, like you, found myself drawn
    to the "forbidden."

Your masterpiece is
    <u>A Streetcar Named Desire</u> and
giving us that great line,
    "I always rely on the kindness of strangers."

THE TEACHER WHO LOST HIS COOL

Mr. Lassie was his name
    and he taught science
at John Deere Junior High.

He was striking in his
    appearance --
a short but lean, muscular guy
    with a mischievous smile.

It was well known
    that he had served
as a medic in the
    South Pacific in W.W. II

He was a guy's guy,
    who understood what a boy
experiences as he
    becomes a man.

You felt you could approach him
    outside the classroom
with the confidence that
    he would keep your secrets.

I even showed him a
    naked lady on a playing card.
He looked at her, smiled and said,
    "Wow! She's really built."

Then, one day it happened,
    he lost his cool.
He became angry at the noisy class and yelled,
    "You haven't experienced anything!"

I realize now that
　　Mr. Lassie had suddenly
returned to being a
　　medic on the battlefield.

When he shouted, "You haven't
　　experienced anything," he
was referring to the horrors
　　of war.

At that moment,
　　he was surrounded by the wounded
and hearing their cries for help.
　　He was there again knowing that
he could not save all who were dying.

Mr. Lassie, hear this now:
　　"You were the best science teacher
I ever had and I understand now what
　　you were trying to tell us."

THE UNFORGETTABLE AUNT ROSE

Visiting my Great Aunt Rose
    was always an eye-opener
To a boy of eight
    who really knew little about life.

She seemed so special.
    Why, you ask?
Well, she lived in a suite
    at the LeClaire Hotel.

Also, she had traveled
    throughout the world.
You see, she had married
    Larry who arranged world tours
for symphony orchestras

The company of musicians
    toured the world giving concerts.
So, Rose had been to London, Paris, Berlin
    and even Rio and Tokyo.

She kept up with world affairs.
    Since she was a strong Democrat,
she would not read <u>The Chicago Tribune</u>.
    Only <u>The New York Times</u> would do for her.

Her suite was filled with moments
    that she had gathered --
a statue of Buddha, an ebony African
    figure, a fan from Japan,
And large vases from China.

She had seen some of the world
    of the world and had strong views about them.
"F.D.R. was the most charming man I ever met."
    "Hitler was nothing more than a Charlie
Chaplin doing a stand-up routine."
    "Mussolini was a fat, greasy pig."

One of the things she loved to do
    when I would visit was to get out
her large box of family photographs
    and tell all the skeleton stories.

I can hear her now:
    "Maude's husband was a bootlegger."
"Clarence got syphilis and had to be
    committed to an asylum."
"Alice was so dumb that she went off to
    Reno to join her no good husband
who was a professional gambler."

Rose was very much against
    a burial of a body.
So, when Larry died, she
    had him placed in a
niche at our local mausoleum.

Then, to my surprise, she
    said that she had seen Larry.
I listened as she described how
    the casket was rolled out
of the niche.

She described how the lid was lifted
    and then said, "Larry was just the same.
He looked so nice in his pin-stripped suit
    and his polkadot bow tie."

Aunt Rose was quite a
   colorful character.
She is now in a "drawer" next
   to Larry.

I've never had the urge
   to go and see her again.
I'm quite content to
   remember her exotic suite,
where she voiced her strong opinions,
   told all the family secrets,
and made me feel like a world
   traveler.

A SALUTE TO A BRAVE LESBIAN

Delores was her name
    and she came into
this world and was confronted
    with challenges
not of her making.

She was born to an
    unwed mother
and then adopted by a
    couple who had lost
an infant son.

While her parents loved
    her, they also told
her over and over that they
    had wanted a son.

Delores was never told that
    she had been adopted.
But, it became clear to those
    around her that she had
been or that something was very
    wrong.

Why you ask?
    Well, for one thing she
was very tall and looked nothing
    like her parents.

By the age of 17,
    She was 6'3" tall
and was described as
    being "handsome."

As a child to please
        her parents she liked
to dress up like a boy
        and act like a son.

She went out for all
        sorts of sports - -
baseball, tennis, track and
        even basketball and
wrestling.

After she graduated from
        high school,
She joined the Waves much to
        the delight of her parents.

It was then that she
        learned the truth.
It came out during the
        enlistment process.

Was she upset?
        you bet she was.
But, she learned to
        cope and move on.
Besides, there was a war to win.

So, Delores was sent
        to the Pacific theatre
of the war and served
        with honor and courage.

She saw a lot of terrible
        things out there
as our troops skipped-hooped
        from one island to another.

As a Wave she did what she could
	to help and comfort
our wounded soldiers and others.
	she was awarded medals
of honor to reward her for her efforts.

She never talked about it - -
	but once in a while tears would
fill up her eyes as a word or
	action would bring back
dark echoed and shadows of battles.

During the war she met and
	fell in love with
another gal who had experienced
	many of the things that
Delores had faced.

They found good jobs and set up
	housekeeping in San Francisco
and later took in Delores' mother
	after she lost her husband.

Delores never held grudges or
	spoke of what might have been.
No, she took each day as it came and
	was thankful she had found a
"wife" who truly loved her.

When she was told that she had cancer
	and did not have long to live,
she got busy and took her mother back to
	Iowa to be with kinfolk.

She was so efficient that she paid
        for the care and burial
for her mother so that other relatives
        would not have to worry about anything.

Delores spent the rest of her days
        enjoying the company of the love of her life.
And being thankful for being able to meet
        the challenges not of her making.

We didn't speak much about Delores
        after her death.
All through her growing up years she
        had seemed queer and odd to us.

Then, one day we saw an episode of
        that TV Series entitled,
Queer As Folk and we thought about
        Delores.

That series helped us understand her
        better and we suddenly began
to appreciate her more and even
        to salute her courage.

We Salute you Delores!

"Hi! I'm one of the beautiful people. Want to dance?

"Why do I have a sour look? Well, I'm up for a meeting with I.R.S. about my taxes."

"I can fix it. It's your transmission."

"How dare you take a different position. I know I'm right."

Rob dropped me because he said I wasn't hot.
What does that have to do with love?"

"I'm betting on the nag Horsefly in the next race. Probably won't win. But its a better bet than betting on the power of prayer."

"Do you think I'm dressed fit for a swanky Palm Beach party?"

"Oh boy! Here comes my pal now. They call him Adam.
Looks like Eve has left him again."

"The sound of popcorn popping makes my mind go pop, pop, pop."

"The sound of popcorn popping makes my mind go pop, pop, pop."

"I'm falling in love again."

Professor Garst: "Students, if you wish to learn about life in all of its complexity, you must read the great works of literature. And, that's why I'm here. I want to be your guide."

"Sir, no, I'm not a Negro! I'm from Benares, India.
So, barber, will you cut my hair now?"

"Sir, no, I'm not a Negro! I'm from Benares, India.
So, barber, will you cut my hair now?"

"So, what do you want? I can make any deal happen!"

"As a scientist I feel that weak genes must be eliminated. The weak must be allowed to die."

"As a minister I feel that
we must come to the aid

of the weak. It is the

Christian thing to do."

"As a minister I feel that we must come to the aid of
the weak. It is the Christian thing to do."

"Say that in Spanish and I think I will understand what you want me to do. By the way do you have a taco?"

"Say that in Spanish and I think I will understand what you want me to do. By the way do you have a taco?"

Loudspeaker: "Sorry ladies and gentlemen shit just happened."

Loudspeaker: "Sorry ladies and gentlemen shit just happened."

PERCEPTIONS FROM ECHOES AND SHADOWS

So what thoughts should I leave you as we end our journey through this collection of echoes and shadows of those of the past?

One thing for sure is that life is quite a mystery. We are confronted by so many questions. How did we get on this planet? Why are we here? What is it all about?

Some find answers and comfort in religion. Others find it in loving relations with family, friends and pets. Some become totally involved in a very important cause. Many find it in humor. Yes, they truly believe that a good laugh helps end the pain and keeps the doctor away. Others create a persona and hide behind it so they can cope. Finally, there are the more rational ones who are quite content to rely on science and to leave many questions unanswered knowing that future scientific discoveries will give human kind the answers.

One thing that is certain is that it takes courage to live. I've seen how the great ones have done it.

I remember seeing Franklin D. Roosevelt with my parents when he made a speech in Chicago dedicating the Outer Drive Bridge in Chicago. I remember his wide smile, his confident voice echoing throughout the Chicago River Valley and his friendly rapport with the people. Knowing what we know now about his disabilities that was a courageous performance.

I also remember seeing Harry S. Truman deal with a hostile audience. It was in 1952 and he was touring the country by train and making speeches in support of Adlai Stevenson. When he stopped in Moline, Illinois at the train station, I was there when a few men started throwing eggs at him. I remember how he stood his ground. He said, "Listen, I am your president. I have a few things to say and then I will be on my way. You will listen to me if only that you respect my office as President of the United States." The egg throwing stopped and the audience was quiet. That took guts -- yes it was an example of courage.

In 1960 I was part of a group that supported John F. Kennedy. We called his headquarters to see if he could make a side trip to Champaign,

Illinois to speak to students at the University of Illinois. We were told that he would be happy to come.

I remember how excited I was as he toured the campus in a convertible. He looked so healthy -- robust, tan and oh so friendly with his radiant smile and waves to the crowd. He would order the driver to stop many times so he could shake hands with the young college students. Again, like F.D.R. he gave a great performance in covering up his disabilities.

Finally, I remember meeting and hearing another great one -- Eleanor Roosevelt. She came to the campus to speak on behalf of J.F.K.

By that time she was about 76 and seemed thin and frail. But, after she was introduced, she got up quickly and went to the podium. She said, "I'm not going to give a speech. I am here to answer any and all questions that you may have." So, for the next hour, that's what she did. Considering that she had serious questions about J.F.K.'s experience for the presidency, you have to admire her loyalty to the Democratic Party and her acceptance of its decision to nominate such an untried young man as J.F.K. But, she had learned from living that one must at times accept difficult happenings and move on with courage.

Yes it takes courage to deal with the ups and downs of life. Bad things happen to good people and good things — indeed, wonderful things — happen to evil people.

ABOUT THE AUTHOR

Buddy G. Webb as a child in 1939

B.G. Webb was born in Moline, Illinois in 1935 and graduated from Moline High School in 1953. He earned a B.A. in history from Augustana College in 1957. Later, he attended the University of Illinois and earned a M.A. in history in 1959. He taught social studies for thirty-three years, mainly at Webster Groves High School in St. Louis County.

During his years as a teacher, he wrote five articles for various professional journals about some of his creative courses and teaching methods. The most acclaimed one was entitled, "Teaching Students How To Change Their Communities," <u>School and Community</u> (Nov. 1975).

After he retired, he joined a writing group through the Oasis Program. That experience encouraged him to write and publish several books.

In 1998 he wrote a novel entitled, <u>HOME FRONT DIARY - 1944</u> which was loosely based on his upbringing in Moline during World War II.

In 2005 he brought out a book entitled, <u>VOICES AND SHADOWS OF OLD MOLINE - 1935 - 1955</u>. It included the better pieces that he had written about his home town.

In 2007 <u>Up Close and Very Personal</u> was published. It includes many personal inner thoughts about himself and life.

Printed in the United States
By Bookmasters